D0114660

MADONNA ANNO DOMINI

MADONNA ANNO DOMINI

poems • joshua clover

LOUISIANA STATE UNIVERSITY PRESS

baton rouge and london   1997

Designer: Michele Myatt
Typeface: Adobe Garamond
Printer and binder: Thomson-Shore, Inc.

Carol Clover, Margo Hejira, Benjamin Hollow, Greta Kaplan, Joy Nolan, Jennifer Rogers, Louis-Georges Schwartz, and Stephen Smith: thanks for the coffee. Grateful acknowledgment is also made to the Copernicus Society, the Eric Mathieu King Fund, the Fine Arts Work Center in Provincetown, the National Endowment for the Arts, "Spanish Bombs," Whole Foods in Berkeley, and to the editors and readers of the following journals, in which these poems first appeared, sometimes in slightly different versions: *Agni*, "There is the body lying in state"; *American Poet*, "The institute for social change"; *American Poetry Review*, "Analysis of bathtub panopticon, or hybrids of indexes & of cosmologies," "Bathtub panopticon," "Blue louise," *"El periférico*, or sleep," "Royal"; *Boston Review*, "Family romance," "Map of the city," "1/23/91," "The orchid project"; *Colorado Review*, "Jack's boat," "Radiant city," "Remarks on the word *lucrative*," "Romeoville & joliet," "Social studies," "Union pacific"; *Denver Quarterly*, "Field effect"; *The Iowa Review*, "Hunger in st. petersburg," "The map room," "The nevada glassworks," "The novel," "1/16/91," "1/20/91," "The plaza: trotsky in exile"; *New American Writing*, "A day in town," "A portrait of the empire as a young boy," "Zealous"; *Poetry Flash*, "The autumn alphabets (3)"; *Sonora Review*, "Totenbuch"; *Threepenny Review*, "Unset"; *Volt*, "Orchid," "Orchid and eurydice"; *ZYZZYVA*, "Ibarra," "Stories about mecca normal."

"The map room" has been selected to appear in *Best American Poetry 1997*.

Library of Congress Cataloging-in-Publication Data
Clover, Joshua.
    Madonna anno domini: poems / by Joshua Clover.
      p. cm.
    ISBN 0-8071-2147-9 (c: alk. paper). —ISBN 0-8071-2148-7 (p: alk. paper)
    I. Title.
PS3553.L667M34 1997   96-45285
811' .54—dc21   CIP

The paper in this book meets the guidelines for permanence and durability of the Committee on Production Guidelines for Book Longevity of the Council on Library Resources. ∞

for George Starbuck

Money and rain belong together. The weather itself is an index of the state of this world. Bliss is cloudless, knows no weather. There also comes a cloudless realm of perfect goods, on which no money falls.

—Walter Benjamin

CONTENTS

The nevada glassworks   1

Bathtub panopticon   3

1/16/91   4

1/20/91   6

1/23/91   7

Blue louise   8

There is the body lying in state   10

Totenbuch   12

The autumn alphabets (3)   14

A day in town   15

Analysis of bathtub panopticon,

    or hybrids of indexes & of cosmologies   17

Unset   18

Ouro prêto   21

Orchid   22

Orchid & eurydice   23

The orchid project   24

Royal   26

Miranda writes   28

Dead sea scroll   30

Hunger in st. petersburg   31

The plaza: trotsky in exile   33

Stories about mecca normal   36

Ibarra   37

A portrait of the empire as a young boy   38

Radiant city   39

Union pacific   43

Family romance   45

Romeoville & joliet   46

Field effect   48

St. matthew & the angel [guercino, *c.* 1640s]   50

Map of the city   51

The novel   53

El periférico, or sleep   55

Social studies   56

The institute for social change   58

Remarks on the word *lucrative*   59

Zealous   62

The map room   63

"Je m'appelle Felix et je suis joyeux . . ."   64

Jack's boat   68

MADONNA ANNO DOMINI

THE NEVADA GLASSWORKS

Ka-Boom! They're making glass in Nevada!
Figure August, 1953,
mom's 13, it's hot as a simile.
Ker-Pow! Transmutation in Nevada!
Imagine mom: pre-postModern new teen,
innocent for Elvis, ditto "Korean
conflict," John Paul George Ringo Viet Nam.
Mom's one state west of the glassworks, she's
in a tree / K*I*S*S*I*N*G,
lurid cartoon-colored kisses. Ka-Blam!
They're blowing peacock-tinted New World glass
in southern Nevada, the alchemists
& architects of mom's duck-&-cover
adolescence, they're making Las Vegas
turn to gold—real neon gold—in the blast
furnace heat that reaches clear to Clover
Ranch in dry Central Valley: O the dust—
It is the Golden State! O the landscape—
dreaming of James Dean! O mom in a tree
close-range kissing as in Nevada just
now they're making crazy ground-zero shapes
of radiant see-through geography.
What timing! What kisses! What a fever
this day's become, humming hundred-degree
California afternoon that she's
sure she could never duplicate, never,
she feels transparent, gone—isn't this heat
suffocating?—no, she forgot to breathe
for a flash while in the Nevada flats

factory glassblowers exhale . . . exhale . . .
a philosopher's stone, a crystal ball,
a spectacular machine. Hooray! Hats
off—they're making a window in the sand!
Mom's in the tree—picture this—all alone!
Unforgettable kisses, comic-book
mnemonic kisses, O something's coming
out of the ranch road heat mirage. That drone—
an engine? Mom quits practice & looks
east, cups an ear to the beloved humming,
the hazy gold dust kicked wildly west
ahead of something almost . . . in . . . sight. Vroom!
It's the Future, hot like nothing else, dressed
as a sonic-boom Cadillac. O mom!
This land *is* your land / This land Amnesia—
they're dropping some new science out there,
a picture-perfect hole blown clear to Asia:
everything in the desert—Shazam!—turns
to glass, gold glass, a picture window where
the bomb-dead kids are burned & burn & burn

BATHTUB PANOPTICON

I had a little desert, I kept it in the study,
it was a few inches across, like a hand mirror,
it moved a few inches at a time, like an ice age,
I listened to *Cortez*, the atonal *opéra mécanique,*
you could spend a *siècle* waiting for it to begin,
cancel every date, another *siècle* before the *fin,*
who isn't happy to be a killing machine?,
for 6 years I didn't cut myself shaving, Charlotte,
my razor spoke in the voice of the world historical,
my desert bloomed with thumb sized palms,
had a little Revolution, had a little mirage,
brained me with a calendar, I loved the 2nd act,
"Fear, comma, The Great," the white voice of it,
the score wheeling around like a spinning jenny,
the littlebook smashed like a spinning jenny,
I leaned the bathwater back into your cotton bodice,
oh I knew I was supposed to locate it in the body,
this modest end-of-things, you need the body
to have the phrase "to go to bed," Charlotte,
you need the body to have a place to hang your head,
you send the desert to the Foreign Legion: like the razor says,
"you need the Mountain to have Cortez,"
the razor says "the *avant-garde* is ideologically unsound,
Charlotte, you need the razor to have Marat"

No matter how far we back away from ourselves
this scene will not reveal itself as a movie set.
Not the low building not the couple meeting out front
& not the desk clerk who is sick of it all.
The sign flashing dirty green / pink / off & on again
eludes through its perfectness—a dull trick—
the possibility of being a propmaster's deceit.
STOP HERE / X-L MOTEL / STOP HERE.
Because this is all there is to know
we know that someone here is desperate.

By the Atlas Evening News it is almost morning
in a different faraway city—a foreign city—
while here night is just starting to lay out
its necessaries on the nightstand:
a slow gyroscope doubling as an alarm clock
a lowgloss magazine & a certain number of shiny things
unaccountably remembered as planets or coins.
We cannot believe the desk clerk's radio
has just said something like "diplomatic bombing"
as it crosscuts between correspondents & home.

There is a brief statelessness in all this fluxing
where we can be exactly everywhere.
Lovers sliding in past the oily façade   ·
do not believe in each other as much as they believe
in Valentino & some fantastical Casbah—
signs for that part of it all before desire broke itself.
The desperate ones know how all-that-refers

must in the end rise from the bed of the real
& ascend into the theatrical evening
where our false light stutters neon neon none. . . .

We are traveling into the new theology
or rather this is what the couple is doing.
This is the time—finally this is the time—
that it will be miraculously sexy & last all night.
The clerk will be stunned into a passionate life
& hagiographers will surround the motel

& here is the sleeping woman doublecrossed
by ecstatic tremors playing on
her face as a show called rapid eye movement.
She is dreaming (needless to say) of ———,
bruising the head of the bed with its red weight,
the wet winding sheet & this is me.
She looks good on paper but this camera
explicates our family album
until we resemble ourselves more closely,
hotwired to the television.
& here is the one without skull stigmata,
appearing as a bombed village
veiled in charcoal dust from foot to shoulders.
This show comes on late disguised as news.
This village happens to have no head at all,
conflagration *in medias res,*
& we call this show father, fire & the fuse

1/23/91

Moveti lume che nel ciel s'informa
— *Purgatorio* XVII.17

at the end of the. At the end of the
noise we could call a light formed in heaven
or the hallucination frequencies
of the One Satellite beamed in via
invisible friend Elijah's raven-
ous radio or the neighbor's TVs
haloing in concert her blue bedroom—
at the end to this round-the-clock broadcast
interrupted by white phosphorus booms
comes the reverently annotated last
part before the true. Part before the true
& holy skull of history glows hot
like wire filament so our own heads
cradled in our own arms for days for news
can't help but incandesce into the thought
this dazzling thing is no luminous thread
but human hair smoking for rank miles—
our hair & the neighbor's with her blue arc
angels tuned in to the Other Dial's
one show Conspiracy Hysteria
burning coronally across our dark
AmeriChimeraKhmeRica
until it's over. Until it's over
& the invited guest Elijah slides
unnoticed through the cracked door & inside
violent & hungry as the lover

BLUE LOUISE

Zaffer, baby, Milori, *céleste*, the sky so blue-colored
it's almost blue & you falling away from the world
into description, leaving your outline as an exit wound
etched on the air like the painter's printed scaffold-trace
against every possible blue is figured as a nude:
back turned, no more or less blue than her ground
but there she is anyway, diagram of desire, a blue body.
Cyan, atmospheric, indigo, azo blueprint of the city
washed out by this low evening, this equaling
a blue revision of blue around the house & along the streets
til it's only blue & borders giving ground,
the window is open, the door ajar, curtain a flutter of fabric
blown back & blue come disguised as air,
as what-fills-the-vacancy as a bloom in the body of the house,
as what recursively undrapes the windowframe
reckon, reckon, how is this blue different from all other blues?
This is my body, this is not my body,
the one here only, the other here only in outline,
liminal & luminous architecture of the emergency exit
which divides house from street in blueprint
but holds to the same city & blue plan,
the blue that does not leave the body leaves the body
skin-, vein-, bruise-blue, permanent,
a shade, a back unclothed & open backdrop,
Prussian, Brunswick, Dresden, a whole city lit up
with the blue fall of evening & the whole idea of falling;
city turns to color, the houses & streets turn,
there's no sky here, no blue print of *return, return,*
nothing but blue, cobalt blue, *bleu lumière,* new blue

haloing concentrically just beyond me,
this is your body, this is not your body
but the naked color, blue, posing:
blue as an eye-blue eye I look for you up into it,
this is how entirely evening falls &,

THERE IS THE BODY
LYING IN STATE

There is the body lying in state,
there are the gifts, there are the flowers
that follow the form of poised
eartrumpets listening up to the air,
the carefulness that is the flowers' work.
(That is how they were arranged when
growing in some mercantile garden,
we have arranged them again
which is the work of the work.)
We are having trouble having a here.
There is the body lying in state,
the lying body many months late.
We are having trouble placing
our shoulders to the evening,
my sister, her sisters, the speaking one,
all the children of the body there.
There are the gifts at the bedside
which with their secret pattern
could cause something to happen,
there are the children of sisters arranged
around the bed in the form of a plot,
as carefully drawn as a plot which is
the form of what will happen inside
the stink, the veil of disinfectant & flowers,
there is the absolute body lying,
even the youngest child could cause
something to happen: a generation.
There is a carefulness in the air

around the body lying there,
this poised evening of 18 months,
we are having trouble having a night
without her, without the body,
having trouble placing ourselves
in the form of paired crucibles,
in the fetal self-involution,
we are not that desperate for her
body's body to work itself around,
surely it will happen as arranged,
we are not so faithless as to lapse
into that all-night gesture
of supplication known as sleep

TOTENBUCH

Waking is looking. By which I mean I woke
into this—they were delousing a woman
with a razor out beyond the rifle range—
stropping the blade on the strap of one's
bright boot. I mean they were shaving

her head. Her scalp barely scarred hauled
out of her boot-colored hair so whitely
the treeline came loose from its famous color
& stood in relation. Eastern Europe fell
into book after book. That is there was no train

schedule on the station wall—the station
master was missing. I woke into her hair
nesting around her soles. Her feet out there
beyond the rifle range beyond the tracks
were bare. I had fallen asleep on a bench

but even before that she was a ledger
entry. I mean the booted guards
numbered her. At the edge her scalp
was barely scarred in rosy runnels where
the razor did the only trick it knew. Snow

dropped along its papery slope as I slept
& the lice made entry upon entry into
the skin. I mean not very far in
but they were bugging the guards
which was too much. The station master's

neat hand had been stolen by the colonel.
Across the tracks her scalp took on the feel
of a cigarette foil's papered side. Snow
hair & boots. The most wasted man around
would persuade his lover to waste him even more

in the pause I woke into. I mean I was looking
from her head to the darknesses arrayed
around her feet—when the train began
to arrive. Hauling out of the treeline it made
a monocle & brought no luggage. Damn the bugs

When they put him to work
    he wrote that fatigue is holy.
When they wouldn't let him sleep
    he wrote that insomnia is a kind of love,
an unwilled attention to the world.
    When they took away his city he fell
in love with his wife. When they
    took away his wife he fell in love
with his overcoat, and every dawn
    before the guards whose work it was
to wake the Jews awoke he danced
    through the papery stalag with his cheek
to the cheek of the overcoat's collar.
    He named the overcoat Janine
after his wife and in October
    when his lungs began to fill with a nebulous joy
he wrote an *alef* in the margin
    of a postage stamp meaning "Janine,
Janine, I will die without you"

A DAY IN TOWN

Either way we have been set in motion
Across the somnolent skirts of suburbia on our way
To meet Jean, John, Joan, and the Mlle. K,
Our lovely doubles in every detail excepting things like
Mlle. K is quaffing a Coca-Cola and Jean fawns
Still over the French Revolution. The era of
Specialization has gone agley! In the day we sleep
In pairs, crushed velvet and carnal acedia, one physique
Lapsing into another, promising Not yet,
Not yet, *no*, all the things young lovers are said
To say under the rose print wallpaper, curse of
The romantic classes, admitting only later I am
Yours truly, that was pleasant, wasn't it.
Some word, hey: pleasant, standing in for
The awkwardness of "what saves me" like a dwarf
Stands in at rehearsal for the child star Zeno
The Wonder Boy who, preoccupied as ever
By the impossibility of true fame in a debased age,
Hoofs it off the set and out the door. . . . Crosstown, radiant
As one falling into a dense atmosphere, the adorable we
Tumble forth into the floating afternoon and veer
Toward the center of an exploded landscape.
And look! We are the very picture of society
Hoodlums in our happy chignons of ennui,
Waving hello, mentally readying the postcards
We'll send after we've departed, quarter glossies
Of a skyline a-shimmer or the sodium light
District with lovely salutations recto, "Signed, me"
Or "Morphinely yours." Oh, it's been swell

Sleeping amongst you on your ravishing Isle de fé,
We write, meaning every word of it, wanting to fire
An arrow that flies forever like a child waltzing
Pensively into the hearts, of, America.

ANALYSIS OF BATHTUB PANOPTICON,
OR HYBRIDS OF INDEXES & OF COSMOLOGIES

The index-maker has been working late in the postoperative light
of the TV, the room's indecipherable blue, the seductive clatter of
measurement, *where?*, that is the question, *where is the body wall?*, the
aqueous membrane that holds back the world from the eye, that place
in the cranial vault that holds that the world radiates out from us in
spectral waves, leaves traces, this could be a split-level house, could
be everything under the sign CALIFORNIA, the index-maker wakes early
to see his favorite shows, begins the book "Z, film by Costa-Gavras,"
"World, King of the," he's been working so hard, making entries, long
after we went to bed he was writing "Harbor, a forest of ships burning
in," (working backward), soon the neighbors, the ultra-indigo of night
displaced by Saturday, soon the acrid signature of leaves but still
downstairs fields of light blowing out of the box at 30fps, he's past
"Fear, the Great," "Cartoons, insane violence of," it turns out there's
no secret, the organs removed, no place where it all happens, past
"Beatrice," "Anno Domini," the vault's indiscriminate blue, history
returning to the East, (shuttling backward), (remember?), *where?*,
crime scene, sign, screen . . .

UNSET

The day bloomed outward
from the bedclothes of the sun
like a detonation, like
the lifetime's work of the eye,
little red likelihood, and
then things were more visible,
how the houses came to be
built on a hill at the end
of the boulevard we were driving
down when you said "Somebody
thought about this road" as if
the grand design of mercurial
American wealth promised
into the landscape was *thinking*
and of course it is, the way
holding out your imbricated
fingers—"here is the church,
here is the steeple"—is
thinking, a lifetime of exhange-
values is thinking,
architecture is thinking for us,
mnemonic devices such as
Every Good Boy Deserves Favor
are thinking for us, the radio
is remembering only for us,
it has nothing else in mind,
nothing is nothing if not thinking,
we are driving east into the history
of thought along the Embarcadero

which is suddenly named Galvez,
even the road is having second
thoughts, we talk about our mutual
friend whose wife thinks
that if you stare at objects
hard enough you can see
their particles swarming lucently
like moths around a lightbulb,
how every lightbulb is a thought,
each cartoon bubble moored
invisibly to our heads is a thought
but what fills it is thinking,
the thinking of our century is
that the world is made of thinking,
"The world is too much with us"
is thinking, work is work
but surviving to write book
after book about it is thinking,
"I am nothing but must be
everything" is pure thinking:
the brain in flames like a permanent
seizure, like a tree filled
with bright birds burning
near the edge of the gated city
when the sun has not set
exactly but landed in plain sight,
it turns out to be a dull sphere
about sixty feet across cast
from iron and a few of the heavier
elements, it was originally designed
by Michelangelo to fit inside
the Sistine Chapel, circling

perpetually over the nave,
lighting everything evenly that
objects would be more visible,
such was his thinking, such was
his lifetime of work which
you would have done for free,
for the fire in the brain's fold—
you will not eclipse yourself
with the old fury when you're old,
nothing stolen, nothing
borrowed, nothing sold

OURO PRÊTO

A woman in a blue shirt, resinous *cafezínho,* low sandstone buildings
   circling the plaza:
from this a whole country can be unfolded.
Eliz. is a model of no extra blah-blah.
The losing of art isn't hard too, and it's all there is:
Lota de Macedo Soares, the day opens out like a tiny atlas-flower!

ORCHID

Seen in the south of that country's south, near the wavefront of total
war: indolent orchid, windowbox auto-da-fé, the year's acedia. The
flower was not about anything & nobody in the house to watch—not
the simplest thing, 12 hours of sun, summer's cool closure. I see you are
curious so let me tell you it was not a museum but a house. Flower in
the flowerbox, ear in the air's cyan arc, mantic green wire. Almost fall
& cool between the mountains & the master war—walking, walking. . . .
Because I am not history I can return "at will" to the house like a
museum—the clothed idea of it, each of us passing, minds delinquent
panic-bulbs, the flower about nothing (we were not attached to the
beginning or to the end, divining nothing, the autumn out there beyond
the museum-house still we could not come to the boundary of the funny
war, secret heliotropes, orchid in the orchidbox, God in abeyance—

ORCHID & EURYDICE

In one version you must convince every living thing one by one
to weep until he climbs back into the marriage-house,
that earth about which it is said that bread is the glue of the earth.
Certainly glue is money, the phrase "the tears of things" is money,
the revelation of the Woman Clothed in the Sun is money.
The lake is a disc of bright money buying a few plain birds down,
they climb back nervously as you hurry through, plain birds like a
                                                    plain song,
that moment when four or five are around your knees
like Zeno's arrow, rising by halves, like Eurydice's bread,
& still the possibility they might intersect,
you would be the one who was struck by a flying bird,
somewhere between a blessèd fool & village idiot,
the only one to persist outside the local economy,
drooling at travelers, holding yourself, slinging incomprehensible
                                                    advice,
you would learn the trick with museum wire
where you snap the heads off quiet animals in front of the store,
tempted equally by science & dirty work. . . .

I am trying to invent a way for you to buy me back—

THE ORCHID PROJECT

The voluptuous horror of *spending*

Two memorable days in a fine old house with a large fairy-tale

Garden and a pond with water lilies each hand

Painted for a different hue or saturation of hours dissolving

Backdrops to a photoplay or two from the World's Fair

—*The Architect's Soliloquy, Nation of Reasonable Bees*—

Dear Gerhardt certainly these are remarkable days

West of the city of Nameless [*c.* 1794] now

Another arcade overseeing the harbor

The whole property had once belonged to the bishop

Of Bamberg. . . . There was something uncanny

About his wife, who spoke slowly and little

Just when you lose the thread of where you are

Someone starts to announce the weather setting loose

Labyrinthine technologies of description

Ending in the word "purple" or "perhaps"

Or some formal collapse into the cyan trigger in his pocket

If a man says to me, looking at the sky, 'I think it will rain,

Therefore I exist,' I do not understand him

As the architect understood the rounded coastline

To the east makes of the world an apse in which *the sight*

Of immediate reality has become an orchid and so on overlooking

Blue irruptions of the harbor

Although the soliloquy with its buzzing

Accompanist ("the best now living") ran all day

After a while we went inside and were quickly lost

In the miles of corniced and imbricant hallways *I imitated*

People because I was looking for a way out,

And for no other reason but we learned nothing about her

Musicianship or how it might take 70 or 80 years

To remove all traces of the world

Did we speak of certainty?

I am familiar with certainty

ROYAL

They moved across the screen like a computer simulation.
They moved across the screen like complex models & we learned
                    to call this a nature show.
Animals but set in gray shades for video capture with a lighter area for
    the face.
Almost white they moved across the screen like a compressed
    meditation.
But the song was never familiar.
Because this was the only room this was the only room where we
    undressed—:
                    that was the plot.
They moved across the screen across the room but it was not happening
    to us.
The image burning in.
Coated with hair & then a lighter area for the face meaning exposed
    skin.
We have learned to wear the architecture despite the sky's numerous
    advances.
All these things—the speed & the music & the room—happened but
    not enough.
We undressed in the room we could not take off where I handcuffed
    you to the story.
This is the work of the brain—itself a bloody spring or electric wire
                    wrapped in ripe gray gauze—
                    you like it.
(2 lobes resembling the holy tablets delivered into the veldt's dry
    speed—the Laws
                    prefigured in the neural network's burning thicket.)
They moved across the screen howling but the sound turned down.

This happened over & over again—the blue light leaking into the
    room like sand.
Burning into the brain in a finery of filamental fire.
The Laws which do not unravel into noise & make a kind of story or
    kinked plot
                    which can't be straightened like a motel wire
                    hanger looped around your wrists.
The loop like a computer simulation—the thought of the thought—
                    the image burning in now.
We began to understand what they were—:
                    the *Thou* & the *shalt* & the *not*

MIRANDA WRITES

Postcards after she
(disrespected & disowned by old father-the-prince whose sick mouth
runs this show
well-called when we had the dough
Prospero)
steals a car & flees south.

Imperial Highway / tarred & weathered / tired / incredibly cold / wish
you were there / /

love Miranda

Nodding off in the emperor's new Cadillac / the brakes are weak / the
steering's wack / am trying to see things from below / I love my new tax
bracket / the car's in a spin & my belt buckle is on the equator / see ya
later / /

love your lil Miranda

I'm asleep on the heels / of this fruited plane / ahh the wheels / à la Pan
Americana! / O / /

love your somatic whiz-kid Miranda

From south of the border / this last vehicle rotates fast / in the wrong
direction / as does the wax- / apple planet on its magnetic axle / /

know what I'm saying / love Miranda

Goddamn I'm going nowhere faster than the eye can see / I can see 2 shining seas one after the other / /

> (to be continued et cetera) / love &
> more of the same but better Miranda

Caliban you weak / bastard / I blame you for all freak / accidents / why
didn't you warn me about this storm / the cigarette lighter to my nose /
I'm nearly warm / in the emperor's old bedclothes / I am governor of
this state of emergency / tell the fucker the road froze / & who do / /

> you love Miranda

DEAD SEA SCROLL

In the holy city's harbor a howling heat, furious corona, mercantile boats
Burning in the day and until evening only the phylacteried priests could
Be paid to approach, to beckon and charm each foreign sailor toward our good
Heaven. Remember them for blessing the blackened with found material: that throat-
Easing unction your name, which is called Law; and praise, although no sailor had
Left his kingdom to be blessed in an alien language by alien priests inashy gowns,
None had come for the day of warping cedar and melted flesh into which each was bound
Like a gift to King Jonathan, who read from Exodus over the mass grave that our God
Was a god of war, that this life was preparation, and welcome to the parade grounds

HUNGER IN ST. PETERSBURG

Did we live in a building above the river?
Why shouldn't the bees have done business?
Was it broadcast?
Was our building's stone countenance colored blue
like some buildings to the south
& everything to the north?
Wasn't that blue the blue named after the city?
How did the neighbors heat their bread?
Were there many Lenins
of bronze, iron, anthracite & chaff?
Wasn't our honey the best in the world?
Were there many scenes with old machines,
exposed for export magazines?
Who lived in the buildings by the river
behind the blue façades which made of the river a dim reflection?
Could wattled couples afford to wail
inside each other like mercurial children
while the bees necked in the pollen-theaters?
Did they never change the name of St. Petersburg blue?
Did the bees of St. Petersburg do different work
in 1919, in 1967, in the winter I turned 30
without a lightbulb to my name, without a lumen,
without filament or fire,
in the 99th decade of the unraveling millennium?
Who's counting?
Who warmed the angular bones behind each blue face?
How did the Finnish sweeten their bread then?
Why were there no fathers in the stories we told
around the burning television?

Was there a minute beyond the radius
of that animated blank flame
when there was no spy in the house of memory,
when we didn't know we were dying anyway in our unseemly bodies,
pale assemblages of lean meat & wire & foolscap
in the static blue of the Republic?
Did the news denationalize the swollen combs?
Which history could we slather in secret across our thighs like come?
How much honey could we smuggle the reverse direction
through the Finland Station?
What color were the buildings by the river before?
Who wants to know?

THE PLAZA: TROTSKY IN EXILE

                       —that Russia was divided in two
on the government office's map   at the fissured Plaza's edge in Mexico
in Mexico City, "astronomical   mirage of hovels,dust orbiting
the boots of tax collectors,"the   Plaza laid out in the image of
what the brain thought the brain   looked like, yellowed involutions
worn into the skull—

—Norway: the photographs with Natalya which lose their gray defini-
tion Pale clothes & hair bleaching to historical white The pictures
themselves a remnant of Not the camera thinking (the light shirring
through the lens Across the face of the lens) Him slumping into the
light From his desk as the background Blacks out What's left in the
room What blacks away into A grand subtraction Slurring through it
The light tearing open the silvered paper (the fever again This is the
fever again This is the hospital—

—the new chess machine, star of *Le Cirque de Fantôme-Mimes,*
not the lone & false automaton of scandal fame
housing a tiny grotesque (an exile from the freak show)
but 2 child-sized dolls, oiled, *masqué,* rigged to queue
ivory & marble figures through an involved rote-play
which soon bored the hosts, richest Jewry of St. Palais,
though a man with friends in Munich agreed that Europe's
mind was divided against itself, resting in his car—

*—There it sinks into a coma between two thin stretches of woods. Day after
day passes. More and more empty tins are lying by the side of the train. The*

engine, one carriage hitched to it, makes daily trips to a larger station to
fetch our midday meal and newspapers. Influenza has invaded our com-
partments. Our engine keeps rolling back and forth to avoid freezing . . .
we do not even know where we are.

"Thus twelve days and twelve nights passed during
which no one was allowed to leave the train"—

—how long til the frontier? Alma Ata to the south,
Archangel also never reached by the royal family—

—had wanted once to sleep with just
her voice, her whole hatful of fetishes stripped off,
her silk slip dropped over the black boots,
St. Petersburg swaying down past her hips
—the way sickness came into her home,
a mother slipping from the steam bath
unornamented as an eggshell & damp
from the veil of enriched atmosphere
to find the attendants dismissed,
jewels sprawled across her bed,
& a pale Nicholas sweating with brain fever
loose in the folds of her auricular chambers
that rose from the gated square
into towers described often from a distance,
from the western slums where certain doors
were annotated with coal one November,
carbon over red, & burned off their hinges
—fearing iconography her body liquidated
in a coal mine with sulfuric acid with her family
—a skullcap: the White Guard's blind horses

that held the city back & away from her head
—off with the whole disastrous family
& how the end ran in their skin's
anarchic cartography, veins so verging
on the surface of their bodies
—slinking out of her bad blood,
shedding her children's flesh of her flesh
down the coal chute, the last Winter Palace,
the drought-dust rising like water
—but the city's towers, remember,
still rendered as "onion-shaped and conspiring
ripely into the azure evening"
—so he wrote hurriedly in his notebook,
already late for an appointment with an ice pick
that would divide his head from his head,
the whorled lobes of cinder landscape
resembling each other more & more
in the permanent approach to the frontier,
rolling back and forth, the southern asylum,
back and forth, the gray mind finally loose
from the center, century, mother country—

One night I want to read you something over the phone so I ask a neighbor for a book by the famous poet E. But no. I knock on the next door & the next—: no & no. In fact no one has heard of E. Halfway across town I give up & walk home. When I arrive someone has propped *The Complete E,* pub. posthumously, on my desk. The one poem isn't listed—where is it? In the surface-collage of a career, a hole falls open. E approaches from the north, leading dozens of camels. She is naked except for a burnoose. She is 9 feet tall. "You were the famous poet E!" I shout—the sand kicks in spiraglyphic funnels.

"Yes" she says, nodding wistfully—"& was an angel, now a vendor of camels."

I explain about you & that I want to read you a poem of hers. She's crossing the desert to sell all her camels. "Akhh, I hated being an angel, speaking in parables *et cetera,* always on the lookout for silvered piano wire *et cetera et cetera.*" We're both sweating into the sand & I see her face—which was lined in life—is now taut. Her skin is a furious gold. There is a burnished city just past our southern sight. "Is that . . . is that the City of Heaven?"

"No" says E. "That's Mecca Normal, the capital & market town." But the poem, the poem. You're still on hold. "Listen—:" she examines the sun running down its blue rail. "I'm poor & these animals stink. The marketplace closes at sunset, when the police are set loose like dogs from the day-jail. Stop bothering me." When she walks by I see that her back has disappeared under elliptical scars.

"But you can't sell your camels. Or you can't sell them all? Keep one for yourself!—to ride home!"

E turns & spits. "I tried that once. Why? I've already sold the shirt off my back. That's what you have to do when you're dead."

IBARRA

Here is an octagonal box, local color, smell of cacao nibs & cardboard, in view of which we ate & slept, did it against the wall, went to work until the number sign was our thinking, exhaustion. The box oriented as a compass, cardinal points & the room all around it, the Los Angeles basin with its holy weather halfway around it—there were days & then there were days, a timeline undoing itself behind us, exhaustion. A red-&-sulfur box stacked & sent forth by the packers-of-crates in Jalisco, near the coast one country to the south, half-watched children dusted with dirt & vacant excellence between the warehouses, chalked-on graffiti, exhaustion. At evening, carmine slash over the water, smell of corn flour & lime, exhaustion. An eight-sided box, one side facing the accidental cobalt of the Pacific, opposite face to the range where the country behind us recedes toward beginning, another side facing you reading with your back to the box, plane & suture of skin across the spine, spline-curve of shoulderblade, too tired to move much—: such is repetition among the unsaved, exhaustion. Who designed such a box, with its red lettering on the base which no one will see? A genius, a genius, because the shape—sculpture & sign—drops in easily, 3 extra per crate, & will not break, not much, an extra million a year, exhaustion. Here in the latest city we have it better—we have the chocolate. We have the box which, asking nothing, has pursued us by boat & by truck, coarse with love. Dumb human labor, sex, exhaustion—amazing to have discovered the same life again, again & again. Around Jalisco, C. Gomez Ibarra *is* chocolate. These then are the answers of travel: when we got to the West we were no longer interested in the voyage West—

A portrait of the empire as a young boy,

feral machine: fetish of Alexander the God,

the mad inventor who spent his last years trying to
outdie death. To replace his burned library he built
inside my mother's womb a flawless design of
angelic metal. Christened the Metatron, it was

capable only of writing its own history—:
"War came in the night, choreographed *force majeure* of
target acquisition & collateral damage."
At dawn I snuck from the hospital's patricide ward

down to the potter's field, ploughshares sleeping in their
furrows, helicopters busy not really looking,
to find the dead had already risen. I am
the resurrection & the life—but who here isn't?

RADIANT CITY

First it was one thing then it was
one thing after another. We
tend to think of fused flowers

as igniting outward from a
central *place* as in sex as in
Haussmann's Radiant City. I

saw it live on TV.
From overhead it's possible
to speak of *the whole thing*. First day

of the riots but before that
I was near home when S—this is
just a personal incident—

passed by in an old red shirt. They
weren't letting people out of
the stations as of the early

rumors of lootings. This after
Eastern Europe. Buildings burning
to the south as in parables

as in what punk rock promised. I
found this exciting. "He was
in control of the whole thing."

The word is S doesn't do men

anyway. A few shopping bags
came into the City via

the last trains before the curfew.
We saw the 81 seconds
on TV maybe a thousand

times. Enough house-burnings for night
visions in Los Angeles but
still the helicopters busy

not really looking just humming
overhead. A car rocked side
to side as in a carnival

ride then rolled it ignited as in
an excellent carnival ride. No
clear argument—the whole thing was

interruption. She was naked
the one time we met she was in
a friend's bed to be delicate

in a state of some *déshabille.*
Radiant as for example
1700 infrared

poppies blooming in the over-
head footage of south central. The
second night of riots. As in

Berlin years back—we have all seen

this footage—when the Wall came down
the main thing was chocolate also

blue jeans. "He kept trying to get
back up." We would not be allowed
to leave the station the police would

put us right back on the train. We
would not be allowed to leave . . . the
stations lacquered sanitary

eggshell tones. Architecture as in
a floral pattern of faint veins
radiating from her pubic

cup across her hips & down her
thighs. We like to think we would get
on our knees only for love. An

older woman bearing her purse
into the City 60 feet
below the broken glass bolted

across the platform from our
train to the opposite track. Hours
passed after S until I loved

the looters. In homes we watched
the ether as in shopkeepers
shooting into a crowd. To the

opposite track—hours where the

walled city of *I wanted*
was hidden by the bright city

of *had need* as in being blown
away from that place in fractures
of reflective rubble. I had

planned to practice the compliance
position with my hands on my
head not trying to rise but was

interrupted—as in fantasies
of S in riot gear. This was
the poppy vision. I admit

I found the whole thing exciting.
We have all seen this footage

UNION PACIFIC

The life about which the Buddhists teach
That the certain life belongs to the uncertain,
The life in which nothing belongs to us for even
The length of a century, which is nothing: Om.
The life in which all streets are named for thieves,
Trees and thieves, the life in which the thief-and-tree
Is the sign of the West, the life in which there are
Seven spheres extending out to heaven from the Union
Pacific switching yard in Wyoming near midsummer,
The heaven we are not allowed to see in this life: Om.
The life which spent a third of a century maneuvering me,
Solitary, rouged in the fine dust of the Chimney Rock Ranch,
To the end of Ivinson Street in Laramie near the
Continental Divide where the railroad companies planted
Their feet in a bracework of steel and cracked open
The West the way a bear, a holy animal (first thought
Only thought) might crack open a Buddhist,
By skull and by ribcage, the white containments: Om.
From the Buddhists we learn that a holy man may own
Half a wooden bowl and replace it every seven years,
About seven bowls a century, about how long the life
Of the great railroads lasted, the Life of Seven Bowls
In which you couldn't see the forest for the thieves: Om.
Yesterday, I watched a pair of children taking off
The red Chimney Rock dust in a stone bowl
Rifted by a petty cataract of water, one basin
For the two of them, just the right amount, they were flying
From rock to rock, they were almost oblivious
To the story of the West, it was the Fourth of July,

It seemed possible they could be damaged,
The parents were watching too, through a camera,
From the corner of an eye, view within a view,
The second thought which cradles the first thought
Like a bowl inside a bowl, four times more
Than I am allowed even here, in the other life

FAMILY ROMANCE

I am a service
revolver in a swimming pool.

The father is a chalk outline on the street
sealed with yellow tape.

Whatever passes as the mother has dropped
below the line of sight.

She's left behind some yarn & a machine
which plays to the father songs.

I don't mean to brag
but I am a love letter.

The noise which is not an echo?
        (Because it happens at the same time
        as the song but off to the side
        or behind like a shadow)
That's the father sleeping.

When father comes to we'll get
drunk & act out scenes from The Classics.

Sometimes we arrive at
the island just in time. Other days we're years too late

ROMEOVILLE & JOLIET

No one in Illinois could misunderstand the poem
named "Romeoville & Joliet"

   (a calculus of clues)

   so it's as good
as written but it doesn't explain the swastika-spangled
biceps marching around Skokie by the thousands
or the grandfather from the Ukraine who at 15 begrudged
god everything

   (the bitterful Mosaic god)

   & after 3 months in the Atlantic
he came unto the holy dream of Pez Candy
sold door-to-doorstep in Springfield, Ill.

   (in 1926 before he died & married)

He escaped everywhere but Delray Beach
near Miami where he lived in the Jewish cemetery
for 5 years without once getting out of bed
or even sitting up

   Some people hinted he was dead
& this may be true

   (considering the dirt)

He still managed to write 2 songs
in this period: a love song for his ashen wife
which begins

> *After a while / all the clouds pile*
> *in congregation above / like amoebas in love*
> *and we know what they're up to—*
> *Like all the Jews with Numerican Tattoos*
> *each sings to each / over Miami Beach*
> *and we know what they're up to—*

& another for himself which begs the patience of a job
to sing verse by verse—you must start singing in the field
at morning

(the field called in English "mother-father")

& finish at evening 3 months
later while swaying down a gangplank behind
a sailor who would marry you if you were a girl—
such fine features—such candy-appled lips—such
a young boy (really) & it goes

> *Money Money Money . . .*

He was singing one of these when I last saw him
& the other is about heaven

FIELD EFFECT

For 8 months he lay in bed over the
difference between "the bell *rings*" & "he *rings*
the bell." Did those 2 "*rings*" SOUND
DIFFERENT? The invisible disturbance which
is the bell's vibration beating at the air—a
FIELD EFFECT—does it shift with the
ringer's will? This, he thought, was the
smallest difference between things which the
human mind could hold (or almost hold, the
thought-of-it falling away from the *thinking,*
a penny rolling to the horizon & so to
sleep . . .). He couldn't get up. It became clear
that he was the murderer. Everyone knows. A
man standing at a podium reads from notes.
In the audience people nod in immaculate
suits, women & men. *When I am done*
someone will transcribe what I say into speech.
It will not resemble my notes. He is just THE
THING between his notes & his speech. This is
only fair, that he be the air. Some of the

48

women wear hats with feathers in them, wild,

candescent. In the audience is a boy named B,

not the letter, not the note. Another sound,

neither letter nor note—

ST. MATTHEW AND THE ANGEL
[GUERCINO, *c.* 1640s]

There was much citation & a certain amount of firepower—
        nothing broke naturally—in those first hours overlooking night
(but not yet) on the inside slope of the San Francisco hills
    which crenellate in the mean eye into a useless & pretty Braque bowl
glazed with construction, spool-threaded by the freeways'
        atmospheric theater, *accelerando, attenuando,* Dopplered gray yowl
of metropolis seeping into the back porch where Carol Snow tracks
                the orbits of goldfish through Bezier-curved lines of sight,
flight plans in the constellation of the homemade lily pond,
    the way Regan even at her wedding could not stop tracking the dead-
brown Connecticut grackles, each after all a strange attractor
    in the flux of her eyesight & turbulence of landscape's closed zone.
This was the century where we loved the miniature,
    the microchip & the hand-held heaven, at Carol Snow's a student's Zen
garden on the Formica counter in the bathroom, slave to the figure
            [L. Mullen, 1993] *you have to hold large things in your head*
(Mnemosyne's warehouse, the earliest known thinking machine),
        the Zen garden an array of calcula & seduction, silica, quartz—
the Motorola heart of the digital class but still from above
    like a *Shining* topiary labyrinth [S. Kubrick, 1980] of scalar beach
sand to baffle ants: ants not easily amazed, "ants" in "Formica,"
            ants in Carol Snow's kitchen: I have heard them signing each
to each, I do not think these are union grapes, *les fruits terrible,*
        mes chéris fourmis queuing telemetric queries (<u>R</u>etry, <u>F</u>ail, <u>A</u>bort?)
to their comrades. Maybe the ants are a thinking machine,
    the sand garden is *a compressed meditation,* & Regan's grackles' flight
mimics St. Matthew and the Angel: *he wakes me up in the middle*
        of the night [J. Hatfield, 1992] / he wants me to be his satellite

MAP OF THE CITY

16 November, Mecca Normal

We walk into the story late, the way
you must enter the City at a certain time
& through a certain gate to be
the one to whom the holy thing
will happen. Here is some oil, here is
some fervor. Discuss. In the story, almost
everything has already occurred,
the ritual cleansing, the birds whirring up
& across the cloud-holding faces
of buildings as if out of silos. If a man
is demented & can't load new memories,
how many times do you tell him
his wife is dead? Discuss. (On every door
in his house it was written YOUR WIFE
IS NOT IN THIS ROOM.) Even in this place
there's a hotel next to the hospital,
a Gate of Sleeping Dogs opening
on the west, a road where the kissers
of garment hems balance baskets
of ichorous dates, waxy as insect husks.
Our too too sullied flesh melts
& resolves itself in through the eastern
gate, which is called Jerusalem,
we arrive into the New World,
the halo of story. It's enough to startle us:
about the New World, they were saying,
it became destroyed. I have

something to tell you. . . . If *everything*
has already happened, I may be
writing to you from the City
of the Dead, the white-bodied buildings,
then the birds launching over
& over again as if disturbed,
it's not so bad here, I've been
befriended by several beggars
who seem to treat me as an equal,
we talk & talk about it, I agree
with all the words except "New"

THE NOVEL

A train passing through a blue forest; a dress
falling to the field's floor; blue hair falling
through the field; safe in your cerule mnemon;
the mendicanted men; the blue prayer;
the Blue Mosque prayer; the prayer for sleep;
the one ending History sleep yours
is mine; the one never finished; the one
never started; the one broken by rumors
of war; the one broken by war; the one for
for pilgrims; one that starts A train blurring
through a blue forest; safe in your cerule
mnemon; one blue-tress'd and lately bluely
endress'd; one you wanted more each morning
to betray before coffee made you right
again; against a wall pleading *not yet,*
not yet; singing with a stone in her mouth;
the one abandoned in the midst of
A train blurring along a blue field;
one beginning Umbrellas of sunlight
confabulate and fall; the much better one
beginning (after your return) Sombreros
of sunlight; how the scissors hovered above
the hair but in the sun; how the blue dress
fell all night; the lesson and how it was learned;
the blue dress in a field in a blue forest;
five cornflower blue Octobers left
in the field; left falling to the field's floor;
sweet *azul medicina;* one beloved
for this; another; the two coming *now*

up against the hotel wall; on the way to
This book is not to be doubted; how you could not
feel that thought; how safe in your cerule mnemon
nothing did not elude that blue heaven;
and all that time the mark was upon me.

EL PERIFÉRICO, OR SLEEP

A man throws ten thousand shovels of gravel at a window screen
propped upside a wheelbarrow so only the powder
passes into the wheelbarrow and the gray rocks fall to the ground.
You musta died once to live like this.
Yeah he says I died once and I had lost my ear
so I was looking for it in a field and the stars were like a seiner's net
and then they were like a system of nerves
and then they were like a sieve I came through
that right back into this country and got a job and married
the woman the first two things
she said to me in that fiery field holding in her hands
my ear were how this country now is full
only of pilgrims and residue and her name is Beatriz ending
like light ends with a *z.*

SOCIAL STUDIES

The Americans are having music again, always someone is shouting
to turn that down please, in fact it has just happened again, though
after a while one notices they are too small to be Americans, perhaps
they're Canadians or even Acadians, wandering in and out of the gold-
stained church, I'd call that a yellow dolor—ahh, a foolish mistake,
I meant to say yellow *color*, set off by blue-tinted parishioners,
I'd call that a buff or robin's egg blue, wouldn't you?—interrupting
the Bishop's homily, "We are all children of the lord, we walk
with our feet, we run like children, we build sacristies atop steep
places like fools." The parishioners are famous for believing in the sun
as being the big cheese; they believe this all day, along the aureate
or maybe mustard morning arcing toward tropical zeniths
unequaled . . . after afternoon, even evening. But at night the town is
                                                                  turned
over to the waitresses, for which it is justly famous. Oh don't
mistake me! There is much to be said for the dour doyennes of Boston,
the lassitudinous ladies of Dakar, the sly suzerains of Zurich, but
                                                        nothing
equals the singing waitresses of renown. Why do they sing? They sing
because the church is yellow, they sing because they don't know any
good jokes, for example the one about the talking dogs. They sing
like lemon conures or canaries—in fact, they aren't waitresses
at all but *witnesses*. How could I have got so foolish? In the original
plan I was to be something more important than another tourist,
another dewy-eyed collector of spectral emulsions peculiar
to travel near the borders of the holy land, where the weather,
for better or for worse, is always a billboard for heaven and every
thing must be cradled in the skull for later remembrance
lest you be asked to account for all that time spent in travel,

though at bedtime, lost in the vast firmaments of these class primero
hotels, I've begun to wonder about those Acadians loose
in my head's horizons, they must be Shetland Acadians to fit
so flawlessly. They're dying to get out, though things look hopeless
for their side and tomorrow when we gather at the square to meet our
                                                          guide
the former waitress Mercedes, they'll be foremost among the missing.

THE INSTITUTE FOR SOCIAL CHANGE

It's too much, B writing to A's wife
of her resemblance to Katharine Hepburn.
We think of the pressed paper crossing the Straits
of Lavender, dragging an entire boat
behind it, racing October into the city
before it comes to rest on a foyer table
at the heart of the world of things:
What's this, a love letter? Well—.
Such a thing could turn a ring
of Saturn into an iron hotel railing.
Ten weeks later A to B (arctically): *You there,*
Felizitas sends her finest, much blue
has departed our celestial
quarters, the conspiring waitresses
downstairs are named Beatriz and Laura, think
of it! Next year will be a joke.

REMARKS ON THE WORD *LUCRATIVE*

I.

There must be the sense that in the next
moment one can head off
in any direction when one can
in fact turn only to the west
murmuring "how lovely
the west is" even though it *is* lovely
as the painters constantly remind us
with their famously winsome strata
of ceramic azul and cochineal
if you like that sort of thing.
Then one day both armies
pass through town traveling
in the same direction while the children
run along in the ditch
choosing sides as they go
over a hill. Days pass—each one
a year or two. Winter turns to winter
winkingly and icy arabesques
bejewel the . . . whew! How can
someone talk like that? It was familiar
but no more so than the first time
she said and we nodded knowingly
as if we had been therewith
when whatever it was happened.
In this we disppointed her gravely
and she bestrode the balcony where
the local bosses clambered or perhaps

clamored. Docents and caciques: the world
is a fact! It's paved with hexagonal stones
that interlock like soldiers paid
only to know what they're dying of
blocking traffic with their indolent embraces
and even languorouser devotions.

2.

In that beloved country and mild:
six plazas (blue and yellow; rust and palm;
opal and umber; cerise; teal with cream
and military purple; yellow
alone . . .) where they sing with calla lilies
held upstairs the fluted cups of them white
from green. You will have been in love or blinding
conversation and missed several perhaps
they were carnations or not singing but
playing "Guantanamera" on five-
stringed instruments or you were inside
your insule deep and so like a river
driven over while thinking of another
river they passed through you absently.
None of them were homely on none did
your name unfurl in the aftermath
of sex or amidst beautiful clothing.
You cannot forget them because they
happened without your permission
like the aftermath of clothing or
beautiful landscapes over which the sunlight
issuing forth from money never

hovered. *Licht lucht* light as a letter halt
of heaven: between those gracious two
rooms—the cries and poised presentiments
of cool March in the integuments of some
enslanted evening—a polite foyer
held open for coincidence as when
two bands racing to the yellow plaza
bump on a street corner and the jostled
accordions play the opening
strains of "Pocahontas" (a wave inter-
fering with another wave as is
music's habit—as when the thought of some
one has come into your head and just then . . .
I remember a house where all were good:

renounce, renounce). Panorama and trace Felizitas
I see you are wearing the vestiges of my village.

ZEALOUS

A genie serves a continental breakfast, angel brings the desired—
Broken golden morning, the gabled mnemon called by my keeper
Castle Fifth of May, *a house where all were good,*
Dream into architecture, Adriatic angles and carmine eaves, salt white
Eastern wall holding forth on the copper sea. I came
For the waters, splash splash. Was a charmed thought to
Grow old here, sun *like the trace of the potter's*
Hand on the glazed surface clinging to the copper body
In the sea, a daily letter over coffee beginning Dear
John, Friend: always here the praise-singing, shit-work, *dusting off the*
Kingdoms of the world, dawn's *jeunesse dorée* down to the
Last chapter of erotism. Have arrived via no fault of
Mine, as one in turning away from everything else comes
Nonetheless to this deserted, this three-gated house, the sea-broken sequence
Of the new New World. You will have found this
Page some shaking, lucent years on earth since its music
Quit me. Each of us will appear to the other
Reading right to left, as through a looking-glass but spectral,
Shrouded in white paper, bond between us, the world of
Things held in abeyance, the music of my keeper an
Urgent repetition against the eastern wall, *quit me, quit me,*
Very well. A cloud floats by looking exactly like a
Word, a boat looking for all the world like a
Xebec, perhaps this is the Mediterranean? You won't tell me,
You're a ghost, la la la la la la la.

THE MAP ROOM

We moved into a house with 6 rooms: the Bedroom,
the Map Room, the Vegas Room, Cities
in the Flood Plains, the West, & the Room Which Contains All
of Mexico. We honeymooned in the Vegas Room where
lounge acts wasted our precious time. Then there was the junta's
high command, sick dogs of the Map Room, heel-
prints everywhere, pushing model armies into the unfurnished
West. At night: stories of their abandoned homes in the Cities
in the Flood Plains, how they had loved each other
mercilessly, in rusting cars, until the drive-in went under.
From the Bedroom we called the decorator & demanded
a figurehead . . . the one true diva to be had
in All of Mexico: Maria Felix [star of *The Devourer,* star
of *The Lady General*]. Nightly in Vegas, "It's Not Unusual"
or the Sex Pistols medley. Nothing ever comes back
from the West, it's a one-way door, a one-shot deal,—
the one room we never slept in together. My wife
wants to rename it The Ugly Truth. I love my wife for her
wonderful, light, creamy, highly reflective skin;
if there's an illumination from the submerged Cities,
that's her. She suspects me of certain acts involving Maria Felix,
the gambling debts mount . . . but when she sends the junta off to Bed
we rendezvous in the Map Room & sprawl across the New World
with our heads to the West. I sing her romantic melodies from the Room
Which Contains All of Mexico, tunes which keep arriving
like heaven, in waves of raw data, & though I wrote
none of the songs myself & can't pronounce them, these are my
    greatest hits

"Je m'appelle Felix et je suis joyeux . . ."

What is it? And where has one put it? Maybe in the favorite
aunt's attic, pursuing its quiet course, its moral diligence
in the lower echelons of our celestial sphere alongside the never
worns and slingbacked fandangoes—all the jettisoned appurtenances
meant to surround recollection and give its shapelessness instead
a shapeliness, "a pile of junk"—, a painting he made of his son, okay
the painting's double, little more than a glorified postcard one picked
up for three dollars at the show while women practiced
museum English, Upper East, gleaming, from the twice-folded
paper, the *diploma,* the four-color brochure (which seems to count
black as a color: is there a problem with that?), "the time of year";
"the time of day"; "the flowers, the smoke"; "the anarchist,
the Jew"; "see how ephemeral"; "see, see," in their passage
through, their *paysage* (not their country *per se,* the dusty rose
postage stamps quarreling listlessly in the side room
of the post office, the capital city that "steams through the sky,
another angry boat," but the sense of having a country one has left
like a scarab on a fencepost in a white field and soon
forgotten entirely, you had much to do that day, and so we make a wave
of adieu to your country shaped like a map where toy birds worry
the cornfields and a forest of family members in tasteless
raiments, bent on embarrassing you, rises up out of the fevered horizon
of memory . . .). And on and on, it's Sunday. Everyone gets in
for free, even the cheapskates. Listen no offense
but I feel like I've known you long enough, two or three
minutes now, to tell you I don't really like it; sure
the delicacy, the mastery, sure, sure, the china green blent with
a tranquillity about which we couldn't even speculate; but why
would he make a picture of his son looking so sad and well

girly? Not an unreasonable question, the kind that always
doesn't get answered. It's years later and the Jewish
Museum must be showing something else by now:
"Ariel Recon: The Photographs of Sharon," and you—
that's the lyric you, who once thought nothing of it,
who came upon it as upon a loggia, by taxi,
another part of the city, both like and different
than the district from which you had just turned away
as an ocean turns away from the beach, returning even
before it means to, thoughtlessly, bearing gifts from far away—
might wonder whose homeland is the Upper East, gleaming
with the light only the perfect know, under November
and hotels in the past not yet so distant one wants to call it history
even as a kind of shorthand, a painting over the painting
C. Pissarro 1881 meaning "Now I've done it" or "When will
the candles and beer be delivered, it's after five o'clock in
1881, and my name is Camille Pissarro." It was a year famous
for its boredom, but it fell upon Modern European History
musically, like the face of Felix. He lives there now,
a single drop of blood in the center of a handkerchief,
surrounded by sheep enclosures and deserted bakeries,
a spent western light pinning him inside his sweater,
his hair arranged like a dauphin's. Nothing about him will come
out to greet us, not even flirtatiously as we expect
of pretty children, no fraction of his youth will yield
itself to us, and for this he appears only once:
that's modern Europe for you, beginning
with copious reference to bread around 1750
in the French countryside, and ending at the Hotel Wales,
Upper East, gleaming as it must, where she brought you
nothing less and figs. Love you learn
from movies you walked into as a sort of chance

operation because they started when you got there arrives
on the scene late, and only so that when one kills
the bad guy there will always be another
who raced through garbage-festooned alleys to save you
when you didn't need it and still gets there in time
to swear it was self-defense, but Jerusalem it ain't. A little maybe,
a salutary boredom that proves this is the life,
because the movie version would be more compelling
and we'd all be swept up in the electricity of great
events, though never neglecting to linger
on the beauty of the rain-ensconced flower
vendor, his sad irises and forget me nots and pretty
maids all in a row crimped into infundibuliform sheaves
of butcher paper on the back of a drooping bicycle.
We admire him no less for his malingering
but fail to mourn when the first car in town sends him
ass over teakettle, and are regretful
that this is looking to be a parable for the Industrial
Revolution. But that's not it at all. Like the bicycle wheel
the world is spinning around Felix and stows us somewhere, politely
moving parts on the outskirts of it all, watching out the window
while hoping for a certain other, or racing through the streets past
the patienced apartments where women and men surrounded by an aura
of gesticulation and violence scheme in groups
of two, three, or five—today they are wearing the red clothes,
yesterday it was the light blue, before that those odd
pointed caps and foreign shoes, each afternoon
a different code, a different way of shifting
against the stoop as if expecting this persistence of nothing
to last through evening—, but hurry, we are anxious to see one
of everything before the show closes and fifteen minutes later
the giftshop: keepsakes for a lacunary season.

Then a night's sleep makes all the difference!
As if! Monday and everything's beginning again,
or closed. See how in the morning the city shakes
out the suburbs and arranges them for a lap rug.
See, see, beyond them where the fall fields begin
to fission: it is a chronicle of winter,
but it is not winter yet! Flowers everywhere though
not in the way we would have wanted it,
had we been there, nor have we since returned.

JACK'S BOAT

April is the seduction of the world, and yet
Language is the whirlpool. Which tears up the tree and throws it
Aside? The king's daughter now
Plays, but seriousness. . . . In the occupation of the imagination
The lachrymose sky gushed indirectly no more:
The Thief of Sighs had been there!
The tree consumes the same place as the imagination
But is not, burning in itself and green, that thing.
But is not, burning in itself and green, that *thing*
The tree consumes the same place as the imagination
The Thief of Sighs had been? There
The lachrymose sky gushed indirectly. "No more
Play but seriousness in the occupation of the imagination"
Sighed the king's daughter. Now,
Languisher, the whirlpool which tears up the tree and throws it.
April is the seduction of the world. And yet.